Doggie D...

Dachshunds

CHRISTA C. HOGAN

BLACK RABBIT BOOKS

Bolt is published by Black Rabbit Books
P.O. Box 3263, Mankato, Minnesota, 56002.
www.blackrabbitbooks.com
Copyright © 2019 Black Rabbit Books

Marysa Storm, editor; Catherine Cates, interior designer; Grant Gould, cover designer; Omay Ayres, photo researcher

All rights reserved. No part of this book may be reproduced, stored in a retrieval system or transmitted in any form or by any means, electronic, mechanical, photocopying, recording, or otherwise, without written permission from the publisher.

Library of Congress Cataloging-in-Publication Data
Names: Hogan, Christa C., author.
Title: Dachshunds / by Christa C. Hogan.
Description: Mankato, Minnesota : Black Rabbit Books, [2019] | Series: Bolt. Doggie data | Audience: Ages 9-12. | Audience: Grades 4 to 6. | Includes bibliographical references and index.
Identifiers: LCCN 2017016407 (print) | LCCN 2017024968 (ebook) | ISBN 9781680725179 (ebook) | ISBN 9781680724011 (library binding) | ISBN 9781680726954 (paperback)
Subjects: LCSH: Dachshunds–Juvenile literature.
Classification: LCC SF429.D25 (ebook) | LCC SF429.D25 H58 2019 (print) | DDC 636.753/8–dc23
LC record available at https://lccn.loc.gov/2017016407

Printed in China. 3/18

Image Credits

Alamy: Artokoloro Quint Lox Limited, 6; Dreamstime: Vauvau, 31; iStock: Jaroslav Frank, 23 (top); Shutterstock: Alex_Vinci, 8–9; Anna Hudorozkova, 4–5; Anna Goroshnikova,1; Annette Shaff, 14; Csanad Kiss, 3, 28; Eric Isselee, 18–19 (jumping dog); InBetweentheBlinks, 21 (senior); Javier Brosch, Cover (doghouse); Kalmatsuy, Cover (Dachshund); Natalia Konstantinova, 21 (adult); OlgaOvcharenko, 17 (top), 24–25; petrovichlili, 21 (adolescent), 26–27; Ruslan Shugushev, 13; Sabine Schmidt, 10, 32; SkaLd, 17 (bttm); Stephaniellen, 18 (top); tiptooe, 23 (bttm); vovaklak, 20
Every effort has been made to contact copyright holders for material reproduced in this book. Any omissions will be rectified in subsequent printings if notice is given to the publisher.

CHAPTER 1
Meet the Dachshund.....4

CHAPTER 2
A Special
Personality................11

CHAPTER 3
Dachshunds' Features..16

CHAPTER 4
Caring for
Dachshunds............22

Other Resources...........30

CHAPTER 1

Meet the

The dachshund trots along the fence. Grass covers its short legs. It tickles the dog's belly. But that doesn't stop the dog from patrolling.

Suddenly, something rustles in the grass. An **intruder**! The dachshund begins to bark, alerting its owners. A squirrel pops up. It runs from the yard. Satisfied, the little dog continues its watch.

What's in a Name?

Dachshunds, or dachsies, are short dogs with long bodies. Many people call them hot dogs. Dachsies may look goofy, but they're often tough and brave. In fact, people once used this breed to hunt **badgers**. Dachshund even means "badger dog" in German. Today, they make wonderful pets for many families.

PARTS OF A DACHSHUND

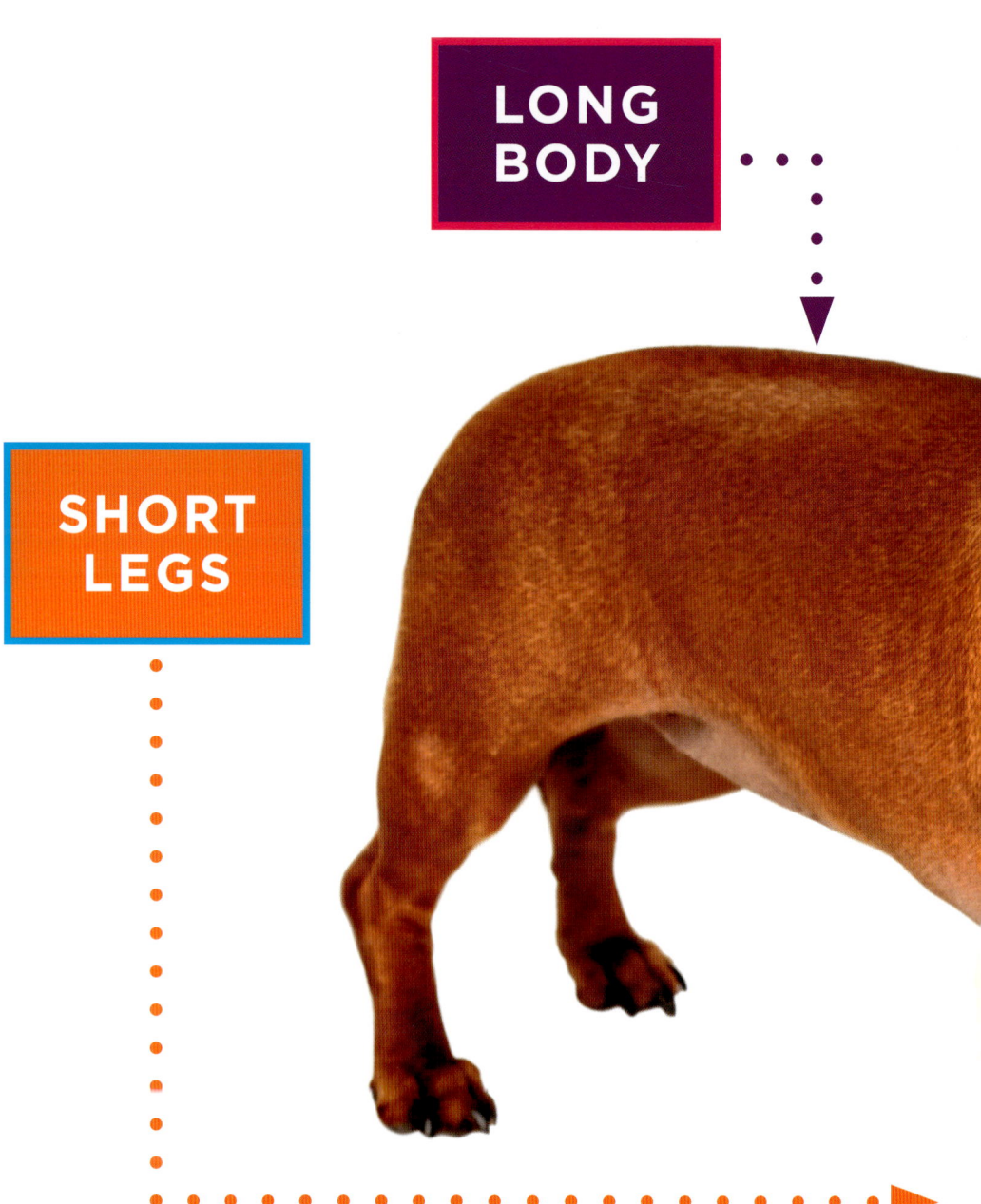

LONG BODY

SHORT LEGS

Dachshunds were the 13th most popular dog breed in the United States in 2016.

CHAPTER 2

A Special

Dachsies are fun and sometimes silly dogs. They are also **affectionate**. They make loving friends for their owners. But dachsies are also **stubborn** and independent dogs. These dogs don't mind going off on their own.

Watchdog

Dachsies are a protective breed. They keep careful watch over their homes. They will bark at strange people and animals. These small pups have loud, deep barks. They might sound like much bigger dogs.

Dachsies have big **lungs** compared to their bodies. Large lungs lead to big barks.

Dachshund Difficulties

Along with barking, dachsies like to dig holes. Owners may catch their dachsies digging in gardens. The breed also loves to **investigate**. These little dogs aren't afraid to go on big adventures!

Dachsies do not warm up to strangers easily. And they tend to become attached to just one person. The breed isn't the best option for families with young kids. Older kids, who know how to handle dogs, are a better fit.

CHAPTER 3

Dachshunds' Features

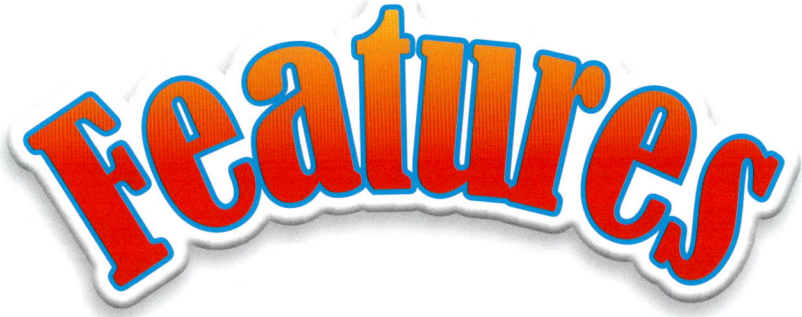

Dachsies are small, **sturdy** dogs. They come in two sizes. They are standard and miniature. Their coats can be smooth, long, or wiry. Their fur is usually red, tan, or black. Dachsies can also be chocolate, cream, or **dappled**.

COMPARING SIZES

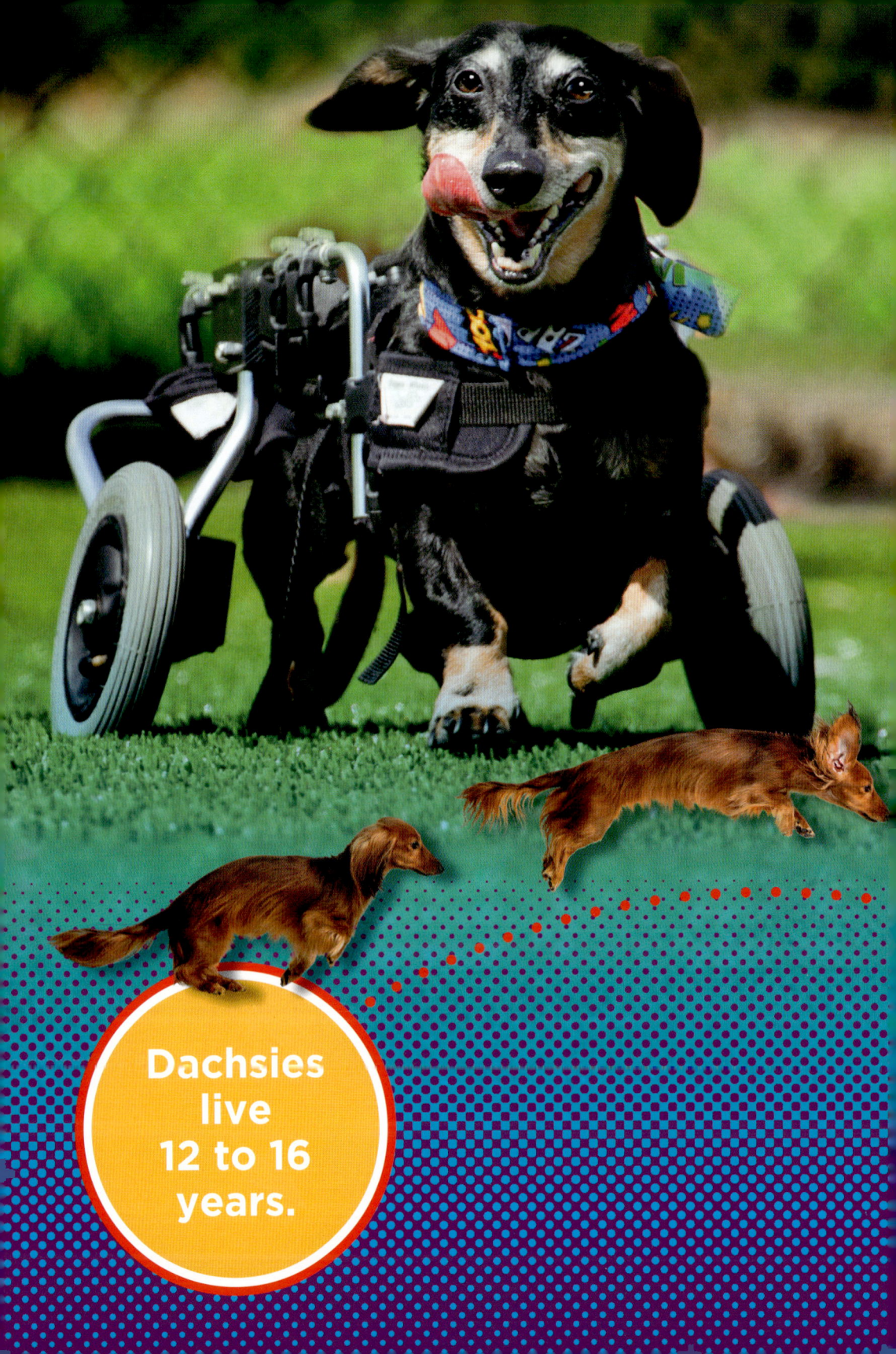

Long Backs

Dachsies are usually healthy dogs. But they can easily hurt their long backs. Jumping from furniture, such as beds and couches, can cause damage. Ramps can help dachsies get on and off furniture easily. Owners should also support dachsies' backs when holding or grooming them.

Dachshund Life Cycle

Puppies open their eyes after about 10 days.

PUPPY

Senior dachsies move more slowly and sleep more.

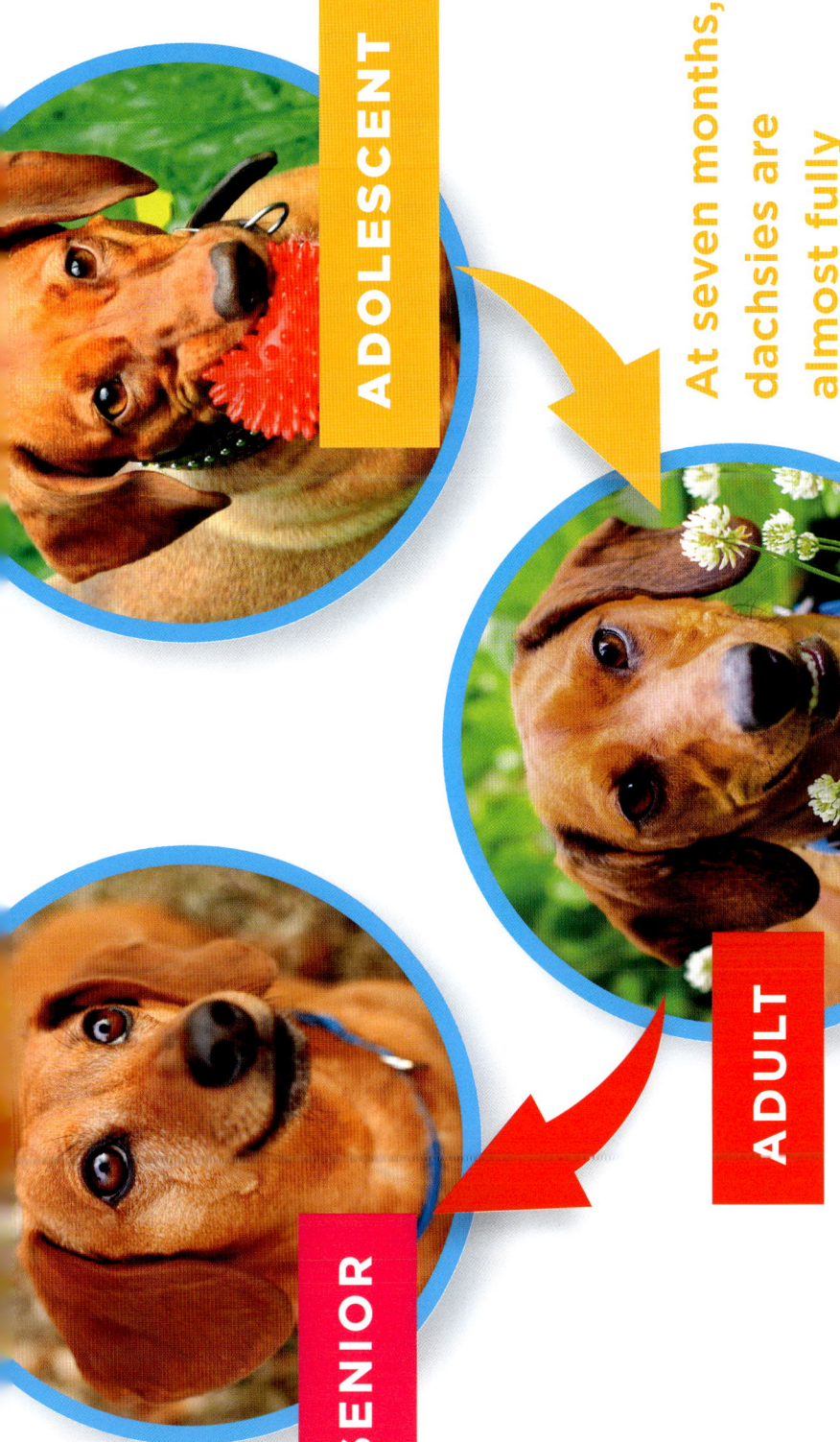

CHAPTER 4

for Dachshunds

Dachsies do not shed a lot. How much grooming they need depends on their coats. Long-haired dachsies need daily brushing. Wirehaired dachsies should be brushed weekly. Dachsies with smooth coats can be wiped clean with a damp towel. Owners must carefully clean their dachsies' floppy ears often. They can get infected.

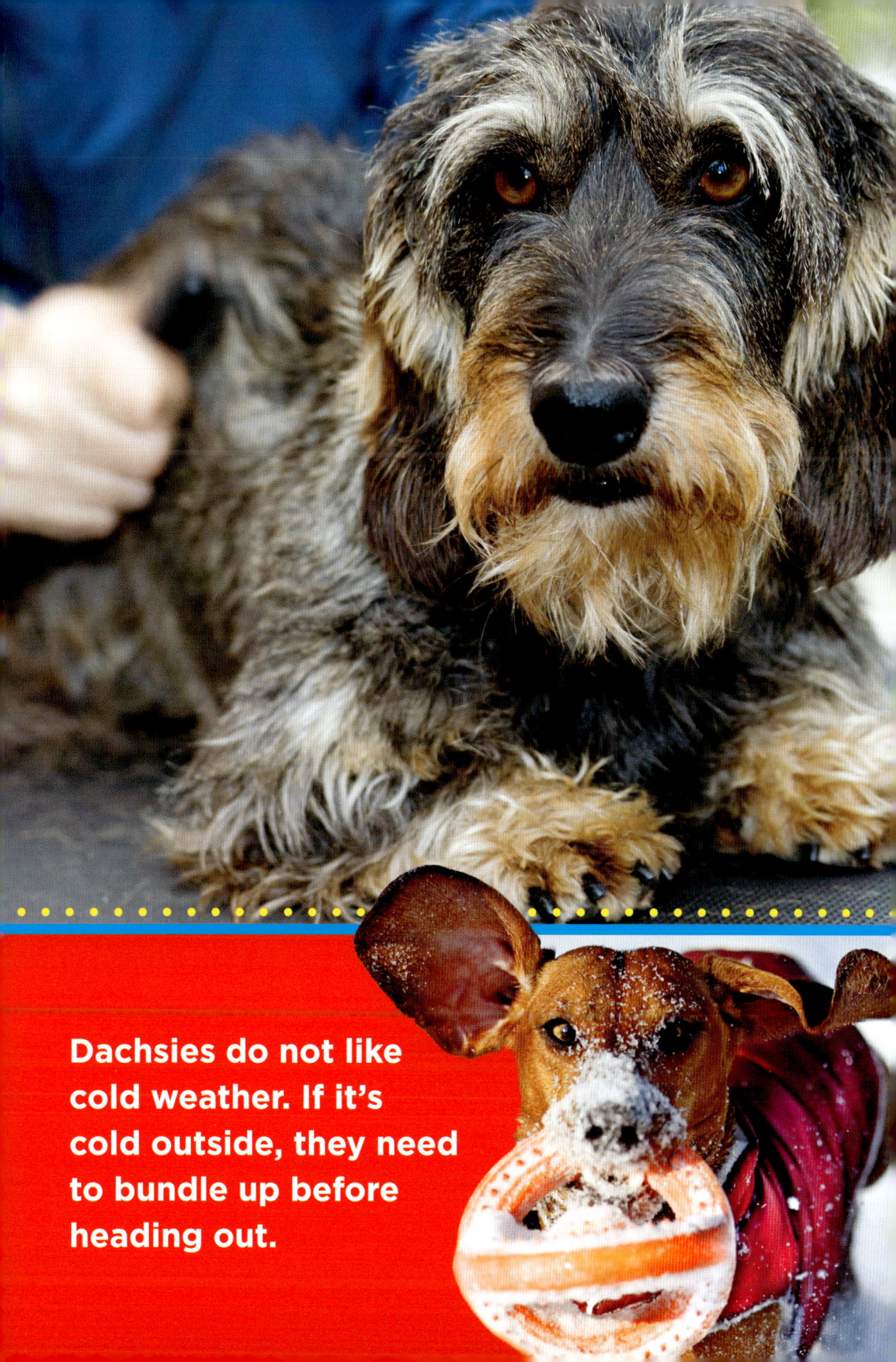

Dachsies do not like cold weather. If it's cold outside, they need to bundle up before heading out.

Eating and Exercising

Most dachsies like to exercise. They need a couple of walks each day. Dachsies also enjoy playing games, such as fetch.

Dachsies do not need to eat much. And they gain weight easily. Extra weight can cause problems with their long backs. Owners must be careful not to overfeed their dogs.

Friend for Life

Dachshunds are curious about their world. They love to explore and play. But these dogs also enjoy hanging out with their families. To own a dachsie is to have a **spunky**, loving friend.

QUIZ

Is a Dachshund Right for You?

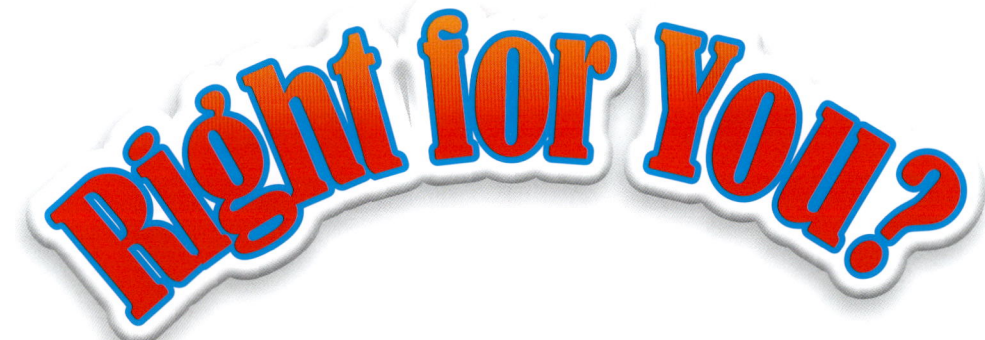

Answer the questions below. Then add up your points to see if a dachsie is a good fit.

1 Does it bother you when a dog barks?

A. Yes! Barking annoys me! (1 point)

B. Sometimes. (2 points)

C. Not at all. Dogs will be dogs. (3 points)

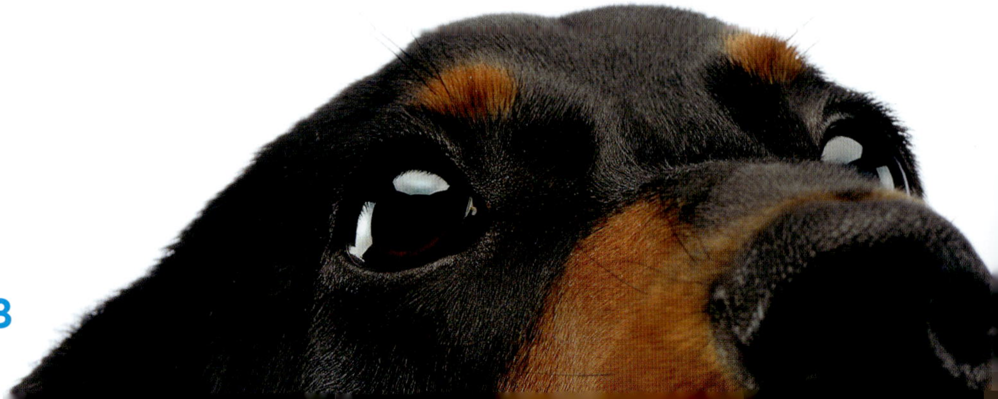

2 How do you feel about training a dog?

A. I don't have time! **(1 point)**
B. I will if I have to. **(2 points)**
C. It could be a lot of fun! **(3 points)**

3 What size of dog would you like?

A. Huge! I want a dog the size of a small horse! **(1 point)**
B. Medium-sized would be nice. **(2 points)**
C. I'd like a smaller dog. **(3 points)**

{
3 points
A dachsie is not your best match.
4–8 points
You like dachsies, but another breed might be better for you.
9 points
A dachsie would be a great buddy for your life!
}

GLOSSARY

adolescent (ad-oh-LES-uhnt)—a young person or animal that is developing into an adult

affectionate (uh-FEK-shuh-nit)—feeling or showing love

badger (BAJ-er)—a type of animal that lives in the ground and has short thick legs and long claws on its front feet

dappled (DAP-uhld)—marked with small spots or patches that are different than the background

intruder (in-TROOD-uhr)—someone or something that comes or goes into a place where they are not wanted or welcome

investigate (in-VES-tuh-gayt)—to find out what's going on

lung (LUNG)—an organ in the body used for breathing; most people and animals have two lungs.

spunky (SPUHNG-kee)—full of spirit and courage

stubborn (STUHB-urn)—hard to convince, persuade, or move

sturdy (STUR-dee)—strong and healthy

LEARN MORE

BOOKS

Bozzo, Linda. *I Like Dachshunds!* Discover Dogs with the American Canine Association. New York: Enslow Publishing, 2017.

Finne, Stephanie. *Dachshunds.* Dogs. Minneapolis: Checkerboard Library, an imprint of Abdo Publishing, 2015.

Schuh, Mari. *Dachshunds.* Awesome Dogs. Minneapolis: Bellwether Media, 2016.

WEBSITES

Dachshund Dog
www.ducksters.com/animals/dachshund.php

Dachshund Dog Breed Information
www.akc.org/dog-breeds/dachshund/

Dachshund (Standard)
www.animalplanet.com/breed-selector/dog-breeds/hound/dachshund-standard.html

INDEX

E

eating, 25

exercising, 24

F

features, 4, 7, 8–9, 12, 16, 19, 22

G

grooming, 22

H

health, 19, 25

L

life cycles, 20–21

life spans, 18

P

personalities, 4, 7, 11, 12, 15, 26

S

sizes, 16, 17